THE
FORGETFUL'S
REMINDERS

ON LOVE,
LOSS, LUNACY
& LEAVING

TOM RUSH

ILLUSTRATIONS BY
MAŠA BOJANIĆ

THE

FORGETFUL'S

REMINDERS

ON LOVE,
LOSS, LUNACY
& LEAVING

WRITING DESK
Publishing

To request permissions, contact tomrushpresents@gmail.com.

Cataloging-in-Publication data for this book is available from the Library of Congress.

Paperback: ISBN 978-0-578-97739-3

First paperback edition October 2021.

Cover design by Tom Rush
Illustrations by Maša Bojanić

"Boy with String" image
used with permission from Kellogg Company.

Font used for interior content of book is Ashbury.

Published by Writing Desk Publishing.

tomrushpresents.com

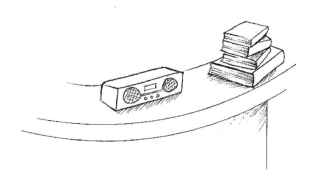

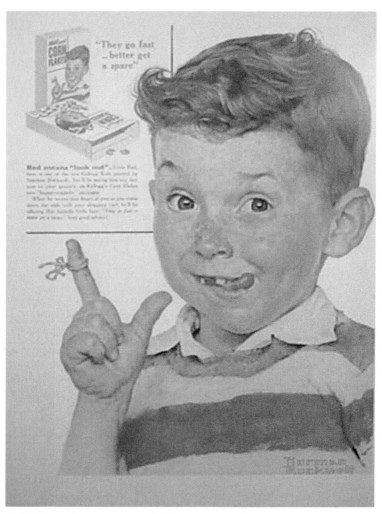

© Kellogg Company, used with permission.

THE FORGETFUL'S REMINDERS.

As a young boy, my Uncle Jim had the good fortune of being featured in a series of Kellogg's Corn Flakes boxes that Norman Rockwell was commissioned to produce. In this painting, Jim is seen smiling straight on, wearing a piece of twine tied around his finger.

In those days, this is what people did to remind themselves when they had something important to remember. They used a piece of string. With the utilization of cell phone reminders these days, you rarely see this method deployed. It has largely gone by the wayside. But as ridiculous as it may sound today, this was a first instinct strategy employed by forgetful people back then.

I've always loved this image of my Uncle. Call it what you want. It may just be me nostalgically gazing through the long lens of time. As a kid myself though, even with decades separating my youth from that of my Uncle's, I figure I was part of one of the final generations who tied string around their fingers in last ditch efforts not to forget something. And that shared history may be why I'm drawn to the image. I'm not exactly sure.

I don't bring this image up to brag about tiny familial claims to fame. I mention it because this is where the inspiration for the title of this collection comes from. The children - including my Uncle - in this marketing campaign for Kellogg's were often referred to as "The Don't Forgetters." Sure, the aim of the campaign was to remind consumers to purchase Corn Flakes (something none of us should ever forget) but the phrasing swam around in my head for a while. Over time, it took on new meaning.

Ultimately, this image and that phrasing spawned the title for this collection. It became the umbrella under which a large portion of my writing fell. The words comprising this collection are the twine tied around my finger. That is why to me, for this soul who tends to lose track of things, these words are *The Forgetful's Reminders*.

To my parents, siblings,
family and friends
for their belief
and encouragement.

And to my Uncle Jim.

THE FORGETFUL'S REMINDERS

ON LOVE

Scenes	19
Umbel & His Flying Harps	22
Bunker	25
Jacket Breast Pockets	26
Claw Game	28
Something Nice (Four Wooden Stairs)	30
Alice	32
Doorstep	35
Tin Barrel Fire	37
Paths	39

ON LOSS

Paris	43
Warm Gin & Bobby Pins	45
Somewhere Down The Line	48
Back Roads	51
Sunday Sunset Blues	53
Anything Worth Remembering	55
They're The Wind	57
Payday	59
The Alphabet	61
Last-Minute I Love You's	62
Open Secret	65
On The Rockies	67

THE
FORGETFUL'S
REMINDERS

ON LUNACY

The Transparency of Things	71
In My Dreams	72
Minor Miracles	74
The Bubble	76
Philosopher Kings	79
Remnants of Tones	80
Have Not Steady	82
Happy Days (Are Here Again)	84
Slight Infractions	86
Monsters Among Us	89
Mother	93

ON LEAVING

In Her View	97
Scars	99
Ripple To A Larger Ring	101
Hooks & Dives	102
Pretty Pastel Houses	105
Across The Street	107
Untraditional Zipper	109
Leaving St. Paul	111
On To The Next Town	113
Waking Up In Salina	115
Halfway	117

ON LOVE

SCENES

Kids rule the sidewalks.

A hopscotch board and broken chalk
are scattered over walkway squares.

Names of boys and girls in love
are written inside of pastel hearts,
scribbled on dry cement.

Drawn with no regard
for the practical weights
which tend to impede people
from experiencing some of life's best scenes.

You're looking fine in those blue jeans
purchased with your money
left over from paying rent.

I'm wearing my old corduroys
and a faded denim jacket.

My rent is late.

You know,
I love that you own *Graceland*
and bought it for the album as a whole.
Not just *You Can Call Me Al*
or *Diamonds On The Soles Of Her Shoes*.

I am sure
you would not be opposed
to falling asleep tonight
outside on Upper Broadway.

You've always preferred
living as a cartoon on Saturdays.

Let's have ourselves a night
just like in the movies.
You can play the heroine
and I will play the junkie.

Cue the plot line,
cast and crew
and pray the writers
don't go on strike.

It's a tiny little bookstore
with a bar buried behind
stacks of ancient literature.

It's a place
not many people know of.
At night the stereo spins
on regular rotation
Michael Jackson,
Aerosmith, Queen
and Journey.

In between belting
out familiar verses
happy customers order
"one more" drink
from the bar.

When they've had their fill
they kindly ask the bartender
for a token in order to access
the bathrooms.

Let's have ourselves a night
just like in the movies.
You can play the heroine
and I will play the junkie.

Cue the plot line,
cast and crew
and pray the writers
don't go on strike.

Although we both agree
they are underpaid for their trade
protests regarding pay raises can wait.

I hope the paint hasn't
dried on their picket signs.
I hope they've saved some
of their best lines for tonight
on crumpled paper
hidden in pockets
ready to now
see the light.

UMBEL & HIS FLYING HARPS

Kristin in the morning.
Diego in the evening.

They're all shushing Joyce to be quiet.

"The sun is a doormat.
Who even really needs it?
Why should I wish what
welcomes me, goodbye?"

Joyce sighs.

Scratching the ash from her eye
walking down ten creaky steps
from their apartment.

Back when this all started
no one could claim seeing
any of this coming.

Joyce was broken-hearted.

Then she turned a corner.

Umbel lives in a box.
A rented-out room where
he strums the harpsichords
he custom builds for the elderly
dwelling at Sunset Park.

Seems they're organizing a band.
Old men and women
were getting bored
staring at their idle hands.

Sewing machines only
provide so much stimulation.

Joyce's double-time,
well it's quite impressive.
Today is no exception.

She hangs a right
fumbling down Franklin Street.
Her pipe's chipped
but it still holds smoke-able weed.

On her back
a pack weighs her down,
filled with for-sale DVDs.

One thing about love is
it bites when you're not looking.
Catches you off-guard.
Sure to make you feel foolish
for even having troubled looking
all the other times.

Franklin Street is where
Umbel spends his nights.

Little did he know this morning
when he stepped outside,
slipped on a patch of ice,
saw his harpsichords flying high
there would be Joyce
on time to inquire,

"Are you alright?"

Offer a hand to pull Umbel upright.

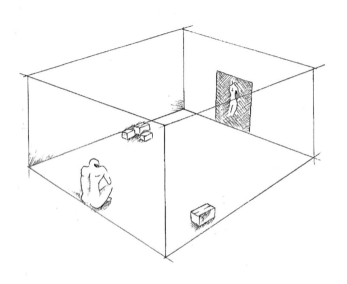

BUNKER

We're all trying to find a safe place.
A bunker that feels like home.
I'm happy sharing my space.
I am sure I have enough for you.

We're all just wasting time in the same place.
Might as well save on bills.
I'm happy sharing my space.
I am sure I have enough for you.

I will try not to purchase unnecessary belongings.
I will keep my odd possessions tucked in boxes
so the hardwood floors and dresser drawers
are yours to do with however you like.

We're all trying to create a safe place.
A bunker that feels like home.
I'm happy sharing my space.
I am sure I have enough for you.

We're all just wasting time in the same place.
There are empty rooms under this roof.
I'm happy sharing my space.
I am sure I have enough for you.

JACKET BREAST POCKETS

I think it dawned on me
on the way home New Year's Eve
at the Clarendon Metro Station.

She was clinging for dear life
to my jacket breast pockets.
My free arm held tight
to the railing hanging
from the ceiling.

It felt like the whole city
was shuffling towards Vienna.

Wall-to-wall with happy couples.
Boys gawking with vacant expressions.
Girls batting late-night eyes.

She had drunk a bit too much tequila.
The jerking of the train cars
upset her inner balance.

Shots of liquor,
scraps she ate for dinner
took on the form of projectiles.

They hit me,
the red and blue seats
and tattered orange floor.

I shrugged my shoulders
to our nearby neighbors.

They squirmed,
"What a way to ring in the New Year."

I smiled,
thought to myself,

God, I must really love her.

Throwing her over my shoulder
I could hear the driver yelling,

"Doors are closing!"

Her head was bopping
against the base of my back
as we fled the subway six stops early.

Good thing my thumb
was strong enough to halt traffic.
A checkered automobile scooped us
in a homeward direction.

On the way,
she dozed off somewhere around Fairfax.

The night got the best of her.

She was over-served,
I was under-dressed,
which was nothing new
but she offered twists
to the same old story
in order to keep things
from getting boring.

God, I must have really loved her.

CLAW GAME

In a bowling alley
aside from the lanes,
funny shoes in hand,
we pass the old claw game.

One by one
yellow bulbs blink.

Light circles round
the classic machine.

The curve of your lippy mouth
curls open and speaks.
You bet me on my first try
I won't win something,
grip on to an offering
deemed worthy of the feat:
a low-cost ring,
a superhero held in captivity,
a familiar stuffed face
from the television screen
or a buried prize we cannot see.

Why do you doubt me?

Sliding two tokens
down in the machine
three prongs
dangle,
jangle,
jerk,
as I shift them slightly
in position to retrieve
any one of those things.

Prove to you
taunts aren't taken lightly.

Do you require me to nightly
pull a monkey from my sleeve?

Turn a toy car from a model
into *The Real-Life Thing?*

Stitch the hole in my sheets
with a golden thread
from a golden sheep?

I can manage such feats.

As for now though,
allow me to concentrate
on tonight's attempt to please you.

Because it will be a new thing in the morning.

A new dream I never saw coming.

You'll say my whole life's
been leading to this moment
and somehow I'll believe you.

SOMETHING NICE
(FOUR WOODEN STAIRS)

"Say something nice to me
before we go to bed,"
you say outside the bar.

Ruby Red might have a hand in your heart.

I know but don't hesitate to impart...
I love the way your eyes light up when you smile.

Fifteen hundred miles.
You went left.
I went right but the magnet
pulled us to middle once again.

Commercial jets brought with them questions.

Now we walk hand in hand on a familiar road
kicking pinecones, clearing paths home.

"We seem to find ourselves together on full moons,"
you say outside the market.

A lit sign flashes off and on in the darkness.

I slow as a silver cat crosses,
halts to arch its back against your shin.

And yes it is true
animals sense your likeability.
On your list of other traits you lack humility.

That's the silly thing.
That's what attracts me to you.

You think you can tell animals what to do.

Like at the zoo
when you wanted that white tiger to
pounce from the ground
to a perch set like a swing.

You grumbled,
"That cat's not entertaining.
Sitting there not doing a damn thing."

Next thing you know she's wall-to-wall.

You swear she heard you.

I wonder if a black cat would obey
like the other two do.

"Say something nice to me
before we go to bed,"
you say at the last turn
before we turn
                    down
              four
          wooden
      stairs
into my apartment
where the sheets are torn apart.

I'll tell you what my favorite part is.

It's how you drift in and out of conversation
as you slip asleep beneath my shoulder.

ALICE

Alice is this girl.

She makes real nice meals from scratch;
Lasagna, Chicken Parm and Shepherd's Pie.

She takes her time,
pays close attention to directions,
how all the ingredients join each other.

I tell her I ate earlier.

She says,
"Oh yeah?
What else have you been up to?"

I tell her I have been reading old Irish lines
comparing them to Chinese paper advice.

I eat early.

I can't wait to know my fortune.

Alice is this girl
quite familiar with rabbit holes.
For a while she slept with a shotgun.

She settled down,
threw away rounds of ammunition.
Realized sleeping with guns gets you shot.

I tell her about smoking pots.

She says,
"Oh yeah?
What else have you been up to?"

I tell her there is something I have to find
in these old Irish lines.

I can't wait.

I have got to have some meaning.

Alice reads stories from their beginnings.

She's found that's exactly where to start.

I ask her, "Alice, is this a beginning?"

She nods and smiles, "yes."

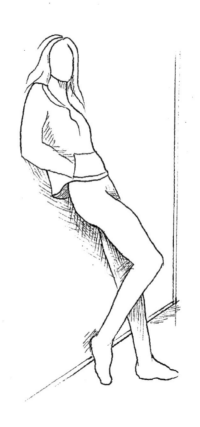

DOORSTEP

Are you going to show up on my doorstep tonight?

Will you have broken in and turned on the lights
but be outside waiting backside leaning
wearing a sweatshirt you found in the pile?

Are you going to show up on my doorstep tonight?

When I turn the corner will I find a surprise
amongst the cigarettes strewn over fallen pine?

Are you going to show up on my doorstep tonight?

If you've got a reason or no reason is fine.

If you feel like dropping by with the milkman,
postman or by your own headlights,
you're welcome anytime.

Are you going to show up on my doorstep tonight?

Will there be plans of breakfast
or no plans of seeing the light?

Tomorrow will shine
between these sheets
or over two sunny sides.

Come on tell me,
are you going to show up on my doorstep tonight?

TIN BARREL FIRE

At Christmas time,
when plastic animals became lit creatures
I snapped a camera phone picture
and saved it for obvious sentimental reasons.

You can barely make out our faces.

It's of me and you huddled together
bundled in scarves and sweaters
twenty degrees above the line
where subtraction begins.

I remember on that morning the glare was bright
shining on you through the passenger side
driving down Route-66 to the Maine Avenue Market.

I remember on that morning the sun was acting
even more kind to you than usual
setting those streaks in your hair blazing orange,
burning away blurred reasons which kept us apart.

I remember on that morning
we came to a conclusion
when you wrap bows on presents
they become beautiful
but there better be something beautiful
underneath those bows.

Oh, that wasn't such a long time ago
but just so you know
if we ever find ourselves
living in some State-run park
as two bums searching for firewood before dark
I would be happy living there
with you keeping warm
beside a crackling tin barrel fire.

PATHS

I've got to find something celebrated far and wide
which pays no attention to the ties that bind.
I've got thoughts of revolution
on my mind, my dear.

I pray they don't slow.

Still, every single morning
is like a newborn's tear.
The only way in which it's quiet
is if you plug your ears.
You're free to try and admire
the beauty alone
but can you tell fear from beauty
when they're living as one?

She says,
"How we gonna raise a child in a world like this?
It's not the world we knew, the one we grew up in."

Maybe new hope is all we need,
another generation to solve our mistakes.

Maybe we'll change or stay the same,
find ways to justify our prolonged existence.

I am not sure
how we'll raise a child well in this world.

Today,
I guess we've got to find a way to improve it.

She says,
"You're right.
I guess we've got to improve it."

ON LOSS

PARIS

I won't say it.
I won't feign interest.
We're not anything more than we are.

Cigarette rising.
Uncompromising,
my hands only break one resolve.

You're mistaken.
I am not ageless.
My fears go beyond these four walls.

How it pains me to hear you say "love."
Builds questions to why you hold on.

So I won't say it.
I won't feign interest.

We're not anything more than we are.

This is no Paris love by far.

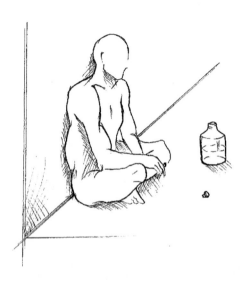

WARM GIN & BOBBY PINS

The warm gin and bobby pins
you left here last night
got me thinking
when am I wrong?
Oh and when am I right?

I take a sip,
toss the top on the floor
and leave the bottle open
because I know I'll want more
in a minute or two.

Maybe now will do
to drink far away whatever it is
that's got me drinking.

Like when the fires creep over the ridge,
sometimes I think Hell is
just a place we fool ourselves
into believing,

"This is Heaven."

Metal curves
in your U-shaped bobby pins,
without a prick my fingertips
straighten the bends
but there are no answers,
only cancers
in my line of questioning.

Like when the fires creep over the ridge
sometimes I think Hell is
just a place we fool ourselves
into believing,

"This is Heaven."

We were running through waving fields
distracted with no thought of an end
then the flames and smoke
suddenly engulfed the land.

Burnt again.

Sometimes I think Hell is
just a place we fool ourselves
into believing,

"This is Heaven."

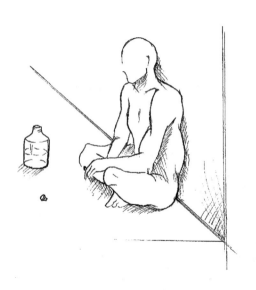

SOMEWHERE DOWN THE LINE

In a Winnebago
crossing county lines
The Beach Boys plea to her,

"Don't worry baby,
everything will turn out alright."

She rolls her eyes.

The Boys' advice doesn't seem like
much of a consolation prize.

She's seen these roads before
with the very same eyes.
Shot through a Lincoln tunnel,
hallucinating angels in the rear-view,
law enforcement dragged her from
flattened cornfields
back when she was fifteen
and cocaine patched the Kansas skies.

Somewhere down the line
she used to think everything
would be alright.

The radio reminds her now.
All the table-side stouts
never were enough to drown feelings
she didn't want to get to feeling.

As far as she knows people come and go.
You meet one Sunday.
Saturday no-shows.

What makes Tuesday different?

The April windstorms,
true to their forms,
take more than they give in return.

Somewhere down the line
she used to think everything
would be alright.

The radio reminds her now.
All the table-side stouts
never were enough to drown feelings
she didn't want to get to feeling.

Years later now
she's bursting through the ceiling
of this Winnebago.

Her mind's been sent freewheeling.

Retracing dealings
made with The Devil, gone wrong.

Harmonies in the song lift her
to places she's hesitated to go.

Somewhere down the line
she used to think everything
would be alright.

The radio reminds her now.

She turns The Boys loud.

Silences demons.

Shuts them in their coffins.

Praying time once again softens blows.

BACK ROADS

It's a shame,
we used to be good friends
barreling down Birdfoot
where Erfus bends
smoking the green,
picking through the
seeds and stems.

Won't be like that again.

On those days
we were stalling for plans.
Horses in the barn.
Icy bridges.

Lining up the "where"
with an evasive "when".

Won't be like that again.

Because there's been years
of attention grabbing heartache.
Thievery in love's take
of what she started.
Schedule's full.

Friends get lost in the shuffle.

Families grow.
There's no longer open car seats
for rides through the woods
alongside tattooed jailbirds
packing the pipe with local musicians.

Oblivious
has become obligation.

On back roads
those days burnt different.

Won't be like that again.

SUNDAY SUNSET BLUES

Rogers Concrete,
poured in 1942,
baffles my feet.

The uneven distribution knows no friend or foe.
Just rises and then cracks you in the toes.

Down on my street I borrow a back-lot room.
That's where I keep all of my hits and miscues.
Oh they're stowed and I know they'll be
nothing if they're not ever shown.

I've got the Sunday,
end of Sunday,
I've got the Sunday Sunset Blues.

It's not a matter of what I should do.
I know and that's the problem in queue.
Been stumbling like a liquored up fool
home from the bus stop on The Broadway Loop.

My friend Charlie,
she's thrown love an excuse
and when I see people line up and abuse
I lose my fuse but before I do
I ask if there's room for two.

I've got the Sunday,
end of Sunday,
I've got the Sunday Sunset Blues.

It's not a matter of what I should do.
I know and that's the problem in queue.
Been stumbling like a liquored up fool
home from the bus stop on The Broadway Loop.

ANYTHING WORTH REMEMBERING

Coyotes combed these creek beds
covered with crumbling leaves.

Mounds of mud
soft from a melting snow fall
stick to my feet.

I went out looking for a rival.
Seems I found the worst in me
wedged between mountains.

Like a beacon
its light attracted me
and for a while now
I haven't been able to turn away.

Back last May
someone said,

"Men are born to fade away."

And I don't pretend my end
will be any different.

But when the trees switched sleeves,
bare bones for a vibrant green,
something overcame me.

You could say I began
almost panicking
about not having done
anything
worth
remembering.

THEY'RE THE WIND

They're the wind.

We're the ones walking against it.

They try to break us,
blow us backwards,
bend us any which way,
keep us in a state where
we're always searching
for ground to touch
with our feet.

They're the wind.

We're the ones walking against it.

Genetically programmed liars
have a way with words.
They take what's mine and yours.
Claim it was always theirs
until we're left with nothing.

Ain't that something?

Still, we keep on walking.

One day we will be the wind.

They will be the ones
trying to avoid our gusts.

One day we will be the wind.

PAYDAY

If you were guaranteed
a payday at the end of this line
would that change the way your heyday
caved to needles in the night?

Guess you're gonna have to face it
you don't get second tries
when you're six feet under
on the other side.

Get a boy a car he'll race it
no matter the style.
Hills will wind
and leave no space for
even the slightest error.

Guess you're gonna have to face it
we were not meant to fly
in boxes without wings
in the summer sky.

Can't bring back the ones
who've left their shells here.

No spells to cast
that'll make their souls appear.

Can try and salvage lost ships they steered.

We crash, leave in scraps or dock clear.

There are a million ways
life could have played
but this is the one
we're awake for.

THE ALPHABET

Lost so many people I won't forget.
Got a name for each letter of the alphabet.
Say hello when I rise from bed.
Don't know if they're watching somewhere.

Not a god or man can reject
it was horrendous means in which they left.
Cancers churned.
Planes crashed and burned.
Heads were taken in violent car wrecks.

Lost so many people I won't forget.
Few eased off into the sunset,
faded old like they'd hoped they'd go.
Life isn't long as we're sold.

Lost so many people I won't forget.
Got a name for each letter of the alphabet.

Hold them close.
This lets me know
if there's no Heaven
we can still live after death.

About this I won't fret.

Lost so many people I won't forget.
Got a name for each letter of the alphabet.
Say goodnight when I fall to bed.
Don't know if they're watching somewhere.

LAST-MINUTE I LOVE YOU'S

As a rule
I like to let moments pass.
The longer they linger
I become a victim
of my own looking back.

A hefty stack
of memories
slipped through the cracks,
waved from the ocean,
sent whispers through
the mountains' snowpack
into my backyard.

Just like you to not let me heal scars
and send last-minute I love you's.

There's no pool
to take a dip in this town.
I figure I'll dig here
so I can have somewhere
to take a plunge and drown.

Wedding gowns
are on your mind of ups and downs.

You waved from the ocean,
sent whispers through
the mountains' snowpack
to where I ventured west.

Just like you to make me second guess
and send last-minute I love you's.

I was above you,
beyond
and in the arms of another.
I thought I had closed
the heavy door I left open so long
which leads to a room
where I keep the version of love
I knew with you from a time ago.

As a rule
I like to let moments pass.
The longer they linger
I become a victim
of my own looking back.

A hefty stack
of memories
slipped through the cracks,
waved from the ocean,
sent whispers through
the mountains' snowpack
into my backyard.

Just like you to wait for skies to turn stars
and send last-minute I love you's.

OPEN SECRET

I'm retreating to a bag of stems she left.
She's gone with her bags of make-up packed.

Clearing channels of the funny programs.
Sinking slowly like a feather floating free in the wind.
I don't know if I should take a pin
and stick it in the tail of this moment,
call it the end.

There are things I cannot resist
like dialogue in Turner Classics.
I lay and listen to the voice inflections,
search for hints of what I could have said
to make her stay.

I'll tell you an open secret
if you've got the nerve not to keep it closed.

I still love her.

On the counter are pictures of the past.
Can't bring myself to box them in the attic.
She's wearing winter in a wood-framed photograph
displaying signs of a simple happiness
we used to know.

Think I'll send handwritten letters.
Hope they reach her on the edges of the West Coast.

I'll tell you an open secret
if you've got the nerve not to keep it closed.

I still love her.

ON THE ROCKIES

The road before mine is bent.
It reminds me I didn't break.
The big yellow ball blasts a hole
through the core of the mountains.

It's tough to decipher
whether it's a natural trick of the eye
or the sun is crafting a canyon.

Suzanne says something
that strikes a chord in me.

She says,
"Time and place are important parts of the equation.
We tend to disregard their arrangement."

It's tough to decipher.
Wondering if there will ever be a time and place
that is right for our equation.

Now a Good Night Moon hangs
admiring endearing mountains.

Suzanne says,
"Plans, you can never really count on them.
There are things none of us are meant to understand.
Love and loss being two of them."

A little bit of clarity.

She's right at least about one thing.

Sunsets are beautiful on The Rockies.

ON LUNACY

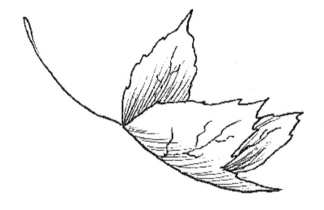

THE TRANSPARENCY OF THINGS

Falling victim to the transparency of things.
Slipping below the thin film encasing all beings.
Every little rock, wind-blown loose leaf,
piece of trash littered or lamppost on this street.

A wide-eyed kid wades into the back seat
of a four-door jam-packed yellow submarine
momentarily exposing those inside to the elements.

A peddler of roses, a ragged rover,
they scoot on over next to a scribe
scribbling thoughts he can't resign
to keep in his mind and solely think.

Thinking much too deeply.
Struck by the possibility
I once was or will be
leading a life similar to these.

A gull culls far away from sea.
Out-of-towners tour the city's steel beams.
Guides offer perspective on change.

A man says,
"Even long-standing buildings
over the years tend to switch names."
But do they really become brand new entities?

A tree becomes a chair becomes loose-leaf
all the while holding on to pieces
somewhere underneath
of what it was before the form we see.

IN MY DREAMS

I live on a quiet street.
There's no bustling thru traffic.
No choirs of birds sing.
Only chirp when I ask them.
All the planes fly at high altitudes.

A little bit of heaven in this world.
A sliver of peace.

Never been a stretch of writer's block.
Rarely a distraction.
Nosey neighbors never knock.
Only visit when I ask them.
Allows a man to remain
dedicated to his craft.

A little bit of heaven in this world.
A sliver of peace.

But that's just in my dreams.

Cause every morning
there's a "Bang! Bang!"
Then a "Chop! Chop!"
Sounds of sawing wood.
Next door construction.
Reoccurring six a.m.
sleep interruptions.

And soon I may lose my mind.

Cause every day
there's a crazy woman
whose lost her cat again.
She roams the neighborhood
dragging an empty leash in hand
screaming "Fa! Fa!" over and over.

And soon I may lose my mind.

Worst of all, next door,
he keeps an unwanted eye
on comings and goings.

He's set up a series of reflective devices.

Mirrors aligned.

Knows when you turn off and on lights,
enter and exit the apartment.

This daily torture's no longer wanted.

Want a little bit of heaven in this world.
A sliver of peace.

A little bit of heaven.
A sliver of peace.
A little bit of heaven.
A sliver of peace.

One that's not just in my dreams.

MINOR MIRACLES

"I've been out here
making minor miracles happen,
chasing Cheshire cats,"
a girl says falling flatly
in an open armchair.

"Some might say, well,
I have gone a little bit mad
teetering on the edge,
scribbling on notepads
every little 'what' or 'who'.

I've riddled myself
to find the answer
may be You.

Now what do I do
with this information?

Put it in a capsule
encased for future generations
or see how much deeper
this hole goes?

I've been out here
making minor miracles happen,"
this girl says matter-of-factly
as rodents and rabbits
race to switch seats.

Cherries squash
beneath their frantic feet.

Pots and pans pile
in an overflowing kitchen sink.

The girl screams,
"Aren't you listening to me?
I could use some more damn tea.

I have been out here
making minor miracles happen
waiting for you to fill
gaps in conversation.

If you're so smart
then why don't you enlighten me?"

I tell her with riddles
the answers aren't always
what you'd like them to be.

I tell her it may be
in her best interest
if she starts
at the beginning.

THE BUBBLE

Busy intersections.
Everyone's got somewhere to go.

No time to do all the things
they should do at home.

Make-up,
razors,
cell phones,
electronics
spread across steering wheels.

God forbid they yield.

A man shouldn't walk
and if he does they feel
he is nothing more than
a second class citizen.

He plays no role in business,
what keeps this world spinning,
and they are of the opinion
a suit worn means you're
a man of the kingdom.

That's what you get when
The President is local.
All the politicians
are a stone's throw.

People wake up
in the morning
living in a bubble
with a warped
sense of importance
in the shadow of
The Nation's Capital.

At a banquet on the hill
the elected boast hollow
propositions they never
plan to fulfill.

Raising glasses to toast
each other "Congratulations",
in eight different languages.

The strange thing is
I don't see results
that make me
want to join in.

Everyone's saying,
"We're someone and
everyone should listen."

The room is of the opinion
the path is the one
they are spinning.

They are certain
how all the rest of us
should be living.

That's what you get when
The President is local.
All the politicians
are a stone's throw.

People wake up
in the morning
living in a bubble
with a warped
sense of importance
in the shadow of
The Nation's Capital.

PHILOSOPHER KINGS

I've got to get my life some writers.
I've got to find a new scene.
I'm tired of elected liars.
I want philosopher kings.
People to spar with on every street corner
mixed amongst the crazies and the loons.

Afternoons,
on my walks through the park and town center
I listen for the wisest points of view.

If it was up to me
we would sort through the conversation
and decide who is sane enough to rule.

I've got to get my life some writers.
I've got to find a new scene.
This one has expired.
I want inspired dreams
while I'm awake or while I am asleep.
This place provides neither of those things.

What we've been left with is a complete lack of sanity
here amongst the growing Polly squawk.

Is there anyone who will take into account
who is really being harmed
by every decision or lack thereof?

I've got to get my life some writers.
I've got to find a new scene.
I'm tired of elected liars.
I want philosopher kings.

Just because a person is first or loudest to speak
doesn't always mean they know a damn thing.

We want inspired dreams.

REMNANTS OF TONES

Hounds are on the hillside barking up a storm.
The liquor man's bought another shot
even though he owns a whole store across the road.

Doesn't want to sip his own product.
Drunks in cars run through his storefront.
Hornitos there reeks of gasoline.

Oh, Maybelline.
Chuck Berry, yes,
she sounds like quite a dream
to get a man singing with such obsession.

Love's not the direction though,
of this oak bar convention.
Conversation's taken a turn for the worse.

Tulowitzki's on first.
Liquor man's on his third
and Assault Rifle Ron is on his fourth
demanding the President,
if re-elected, sees a bloody exit.

As if for emphasis inserting racial slurs.

Children within earshot.
Overgrown children play in the sandbox
at a place where overgrown opinions
sometimes rewind us back to the 1950's.

And oh, I guess the thing is
I was hoping we were past this
then the news flashes the same sad story.

A young black man was walking home in Florida.
He had his hood up,
iced tea in a cup,
snacking on a bag of rainbow flavored Skittles.

Shot down because he appeared suspicious.

Fit the description of men who rob houses.

I wonder what Assault Rifle Ron would do.
Would he feel threatened by a similar youth?

I'm assuming he would
since he holds such presidential views.

He's armed at home, too.

Meanwhile, the bartender's familiar with his curse.
Making money means putting up with their worst.

Liquid bullets of various forms
often reappear as venomous words.

They are the guns.
He is the one who loads them.

In the end
who is the one responsible for the triggers
and all the loosely thrown "niggers?"

Children within earshot.
Overgrown children play in the sandbox
at a place where overgrown opinions
sometimes rewind us back to the 1950's.

And oh, I guess the thing is
there's not much of a difference
between drunks and those
subtle in their righteousness.

It may be a matter of opinion
but were the times really that nice then?

Remnants of tones
don't make it sound so appealing.

HAVE NOT STEADY

My bell is always ringing
so my belly's always aching.

There goes another carbonated ale
thrown down the hatch.

Last night,
I broke last lines of defense.
Now an army is marching
fully armed
and pissed
in my direction.

We'll see who comes to my protection.

A little girl scribbles in crayon
on worn construction paper,

"You have not steady."

She's right.

   I

am

      not

  steady.

She's young but she notices
writing on the walls.

She questions why my brain
looks like it's going to burst
when I leave in the morning
for the suit and tie world.

She knows my bell is always ringing
so my belly's always aching.

Here comes another street bought cure
to smoke in the evening.

This afternoon,
I tripped and stumbled
in cartoon fashion.
Smashed through a corporate wall.
Sure did leave an impression.

We'll see who comes to my protection.

A little girl scribbles in crayon
(green and burnt sienna),

"You have not steady."

She's right.

   I

       am

  not

       steady.

She's young but she notices
when minds drift far away.

She questions why I go to work every day
as she runs off with her imagination to play.

HAPPY DAYS (ARE HERE AGAIN)

They say,
"Happy days are here again."
I don't know where they've been.
Somewhere green?
Somewhere great?
I don't know,
outer space?

And if I die before I wake
I pray the Lord
my soul He'll take
and if He won't
the Devil will
but like the Lord
when he's had his fill
he'll pass me on to another place
amongst the stars,
maybe happy days.

And if I'm wrong
either way
I will be gone.
You will remain.

Whoa,
had a bone or two to pick
with this great big world.
Whined and moaned,
let anyone who'd listen know
what a no good shitty hand I had drawn.

Now I'm done.

Because happy days are here again.
I don't know where they've been.
Somewhere green?
Somewhere great?
I don't know,
outer space?

And if the sky
it falls today
well that wouldn't be a catastrophe.

Sure, we'd lose the view,
be shortchanged,
but have overcome
space between stars
and happy days.

Had a bone or two to pick
with this great big world.
Whined and moaned,
let anyone who'd listen know
in this game of kings and queens
felt like a pawn.

Now I'm done.

Because.

SLIGHT INFRACTIONS

Maybe I'm seeing things,
crazy dreams of my life tipped over.
It may be just a breakdown.
Right now, a moment of disorder.

Should I spend another day
with my eyes awake
as a social courtesy?

When the days
don't serve as a break
from the nights (oh so long)
wouldn't that make you want to leave?

Oh, I have made slight infractions.
Now I cross the tracks and
turn my head up stargazed.

Rites of passage
and a Lacoste emblem
hang over my heart.

I have been a fool.

Oh, I have made slight infractions.
Now I cross the tracks and
turn my head up stargazed.

Is that Mickey Mouse
and Gorbachev
at a tea party?

I have been a fool.

These psychedelic cures
only heal so much.
They tend to lend a hand
then want to lend another.

All they do
is trip out my point of view,
make me want to ask
or beg for another.

Never solves the problems.

If I could, would I walk my shoes
through a different town tomorrow?

Wouldn't sell my soul
but if you hold the key
I might be taking offers.

Oh, I have made slight infractions.
Now I cross the tracks and
turn my head up stargazed.

Broken records.
East Coast standards
blare on my headphones.

Wandering somewhere...

hell if I know.

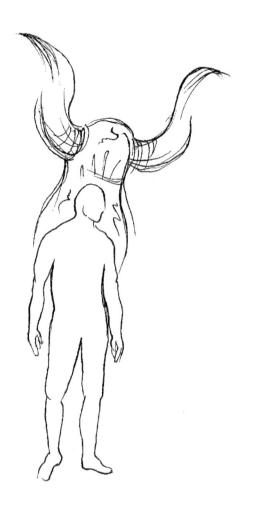

MONSTERS AMONG US

Everyone's got hindsight
telling us tell-tale signs were clear.
This is what we should look out for.
This is what we should steer clear of.

There are monsters among us
disguised in human skin.
Every day we walk
we walk next to one of them.

We'd like to know but we're too afraid to ask,
"Are you what keeps me up at night?
Are you what they warned about
when I was younger?"

Then the monsters go on their merry way.
One day to set fire and burst from their skin.

If it's not hyped,
how are we to know who is insane?
How are we to tell
The Good
from *The Bad*
from *The In-Between?*

If adjectives aren't placed high atop pages,
how are we to know how much we should cry
and when we should allow tears to subside?

There are monsters among us
disguised in human skin.
Every day we walk
we walk next to one of them.

We'd like to know but we're too afraid to ask,
"Are you what keeps me up at night?
Are you what they warned about
when I was younger?"

Then the monsters go on their merry way.
One day to set fire and burst from their skin.

And we say,
"How could someone leap so far from the norm?
So far from the child their mother once held?

Was it my fault?

Was it yours?"

The headlines bring answers from the wise
because it's not real until
there's a label hitched on its coattails,
newspaper with colorful language,
print imprinted on our minds how we should feel.

Is it not real unless there's a cameraman present
showing how and where all the dead fell?

Bringing comfort
this was a monster,
not a man.

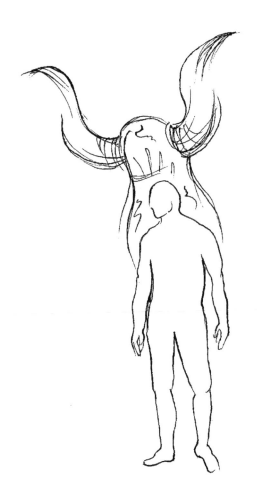

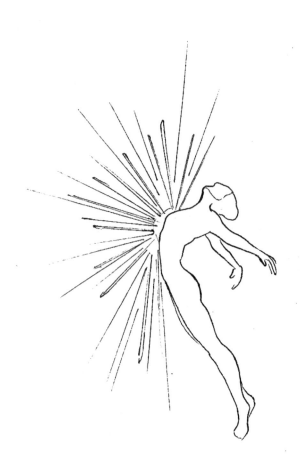

MOTHER

Is there a man alive who walks the Earth?
We would bow and call him Father
but he would never allow us to fall to our knees.

He doesn't need your praise.
Isn't looking for your riches.
Not an ounce of power is needed.
Just your ears and hearts to lend to each other.

Is there a woman alive who walks the Earth?
We would bow and call her Mother
but all she would ask is that we say, "Please."

She doesn't need your praise.
Isn't looking for your riches.
Not an ounce of power is needed.
Just your ears and hearts to lend to each other.

There's no Dr. King.
No Mother Theresa.
No Gandhi to spread his wings.

It's official.
There's no meaning behind our cause.
No soul to our current mission.
We're all hiding behind agendas.

They didn't need your praise.
Weren't looking for your riches.
Not an ounce of power was needed.
Just your ears and hearts to lend to each other.

So lend them to each other.

ON LEAVING

IN HER VIEW

She has stormy eyes.
She yawns wide.
Her vision's wet and blurry.
The scattered dry ground
is pinned down by expanding puddles.

On rainy nights the lamps light.
She swears this place
looks like a New England Village.

All this from the view of her rented-out room.

The gangs on both sides of the street
don't know about the deals
she's made with the other.
She hollers hip jokes.
They throw signals
if they ever notice trouble.
There used to be reasons to smile.
Now she doesn't want to.

All of this removed from her rented-out room.

She has flashbacks flying fast,
flying fast, fast-forward.
The scattered dry ground
is pinned down by still-sitting puddles.
On rainy nights the fogs might
make this place look just like a New England Village.

All this in her view from her rented-out room.

With borderline regrets
she packs her daydreams in a box.
Decides to patiently wait on their shapes.
Hopes they show some improvement.

The scattered dry ground
is clearing now, evaporating puddles.

All this in rear view of her rented-out room.

SCARS

There's a trickling down the pane.
Chalk one in the column for the weatherman.
He called it yesterday.

The week will be soaked with rain.
Writing on the wall's been written in blotchy ink
and it's running down the bricks.

Uniform informs the day
which version of me will be joining the scene.

Good or bad hulking green?

There's no denying
the past lives in words and deeds
and the future knows their faces.

Somewhere down the spiral
long passed the side of the rainbow
where treasures are said to grow
men cling to their bibles.
Everyone has a rival.

Worst of all, themselves.

Shattered mirrors hold memories of the battles.

Where do we go with the scars?

RIPPLE TO A LARGER RING

What you ought to do right now is search.

There is a whole town with corners
hidden back in the woods
known to cure shaky mental states,
where you can go dip toes in lakes.
Rest your head against sturdy wooden planks.

What you ought to do right now is soar.

There is a whole town with corners
you have never known
that may suit your turbulent speeds,
offer good views for emptying minds clean.
Dust off thoughts of all their impurities.

Nervous twitching
never ever
solves a damn thing.
Mostly leads
to a round of nervous shakes.
There are solutions
here at the tips of your fingers
for you to identify and take.

Anchor yourself by the dock for a while.
Spend some time and figure out how
a ripple grows big
and spreads into a larger ring
if you wait...

when you wait.

HOOKS & DIVES

Through the hikes and dives
across the lake the path winds,
a white house creaks above small wakes.
Can't afford the view from the home's dock planks.
Settle for this one removed today.

Passing a wound-up blonde,
strawberry shade,
tangled in a stroller, dog on a leash.
She's taken on more than she can take.

Been feeling the same.

Wherever I go trouble seems to follow.
Nerves on edge full twenty-four-hour cycle.

Like to backpedal
to a time when things were tame
and the worst wasn't expected.

Life wasn't so hectic.

My mind wasn't so damn distracted.

Too much of me has been neglected.

Got to unravel before I cut off circulation.

Two mutts of my own,
one with three legs,
wait at home.
No telling the mess they'll have for me.

Kick 'em if they knew what they're doing was rank.
Not their fault.
Never received proper training.

Been feeling the same.

Whatever I do results tend to backfire.

Think I've got one in hand
then the man I owe grabs his pile.

Stuck in denial
about whether the change
should begin with me.

Guess that's where you start
when everything's
been staying the same.

PRETTY PASTEL HOUSES

It's nice to hear hurricanes
haven't leveled all the pretty pastel houses.

Seaboards hold waves at bay
from crashing on the shorelines.

I'm sure the summer heat and accents
take a short while to grow accustomed to.

Still, Charleston remains just a dream of mine.

I imagine proper ladies carry umbrellas
even when the sky is clear.

They nod their heads at potential suitors
passing on the promenade.

It is true corsets don't force cleavage
as high as they once did.

Still, Charleston remains just a dream of mine.

I picture sailors settling
in regular seats at the ends of bars
topping each other's stories about
the sizes of whales they've caught,
removing caps no matter if an old
or young lady walks through the door,
making sure to stand and offer up their seats.

It's nice to hear hurricanes
haven't leveled all the pretty pastel houses.

I can hear by your voice you're considering staying.

Trading in the suburbs
for sand-beneath-your-feet living.

Still, Charleston remains just a dream of mine.

ACROSS THE STREET

All the people sleep five houses in a row.
Connected walls turn the slightest noise loud.

Left my light lit on the second level.

"Is it everything you dreamed
living across the street?"

A slight change of scenery.
It's modest at best.

There's more room for clutter to cover up the rugs.

Ants file single file over from my old abode.

"Is it everything you dreamed
living across the street?"

Not sure who I thought I would fool.
They track changes of address.
The postman's job is to catch wind
of new living arrangements.

Didn't really think he'd take my bribes,
agree to leave my past behind me.

"Is it everything you dreamed
living across the street?"

All the people sleep five houses in a row.
Connected walls turn the slightest noise loud.

Empty out my pockets on top of dresser drawers.

"Is it everything you dreamed
living across the street?"

UNTRADITIONAL ZIPPER

Right then,
chemicals shocked me with delight
in my back lobe on bad streets
amongst compromised situations.

I would have been wise to reach
these revelations sooner.

I'm bidding goodbye in one form or another.

Right then,
chemicals led me to descry
that my bad lobe and backstreets
had taken their toll and then some.

Here it comes, my epiphanic solution:
I'm bidding goodbye in one form or another.

Old School has come and turned back in-style.
There's a new girl wearing no pants
playing public arenas.

I wonder what she wears to formal dinners.
Are there laws against her sitting Indian-style?

Showing skin has never been my preference
but someday I would like to wear
an untraditional zipper.
The kind where teeth don't line up
in a perfect fashion
or exist at all like on her.

I still put on my cords in a normal manner,
join opposing tracks of gold,
snap the button,
snatch my stuff then I'm off in seconds
to file in line with the daily procession.

But now it's time to bid goodbye
in one form or another.

LEAVING ST. PAUL

I'm leaving St. Paul
with alcohol fresh on my lips.
I'm going where all the hippie girls live
and cable cars still exist.

The wanderer's curse
has become a welcomed plight, you see.

This search may inevitably break me.

I'm leaving St. Paul
with alcohol fresh on my lips.
Maybe I will find myself an Asian girl
with fine Creole skin and Hispanic cheekbones.

But that's not even the entire point.

This search may inevitably break me.

Or in fact rejuvenate me.

Either way I will be on to something.

Something I wasn't on to before.

I'm leaving St. Paul
with alcohol fresh on my lips.
I'm going where all the hippie girls live
and cable cars still exist.

It's not just about a woman.
Been feeling like a caged human.

This search may inevitably break me.

ON TO THE NEXT TOWN

Tried to get a job at the carnival
but they said, "No."
Applied to operate The Whirly Whirl
but they said, "No."

So I tried to get a job at The Wishing Well
but they said, "No."
Applied to grant wishes with alcohol
but they said, "No."

Well it seems like there are no jobs to be found.

I guess it's on to the next town.

Tried to get a job at The Village Inn
but they said, "No."
Applied to cook steaks at any degree
but they said, "No."

So I tried to get a job at the local market
but they said, "No."
Applied to bag groceries in checkout lines
but they said, "No."

Well it seems like there are no jobs to be found.

I guess it's on to the next town.

Tough on a man
without a change of pants
or secondary plans
to advance his social prospects.

Are you telling me
every place in town is fully staffed?

Aren't there any openings?

No?
No jobs around?

I guess it's on to the next town.

WAKING UP IN SALINA

Waking up in Salina
I'm wondering if I mean a single word I say.

A small town past Topeka.
The girl at the counter waves
as I step outside the motel.

No set destination.
Counting change to fill my gas tank
so I can get to wherever it is I'm going.

Waking up in Salina
I'm wondering if I mean a single word I say.

How do I measure up
to the tumblers who went before me?
Are my lines in line with my life story?
Moments of glory.
Self-sabotage mostly.
Waking up in Salina
I'm wondering if I mean a
single word I say.

Waking up in Salina
I'm wondering if I mean a single word I say.

Grown a weary demeanor.
All these eighteen-wheelers weave,
slow and rev around my four.

Then a Kansas sky opens and pours down
unleashing the fury of Midwestern thunderstorms.
I'm back and forth with each sheet of rain.
The ominous thunder shakes me.

Am I a shot of lightning or just a frightened little boy
running as fast as he can far away from home?

Waking up in Salina
I'm wondering if I mean a single word I say.

HALFWAY

Tires and tubes for sale at a roadside Texaco.
Dirt and gravel exchanged for paved asphalt.
A hitcher hiking home hailing help with his thumb.
In those days someone would stop.

Coca-Cola at five cents a pop.
Chevy and Buick dominating waves of the future.

A snapshot of America, black and white,
above a toilet in a tavern at the dividing line.

Halfway between where I was and where I will be.

Bottles of booze clang loudly
to sound each empty drink.

Horse gamblers, farriers wait and see.
No one bets on Number Three.
No one claims victory.
No spoils, no crown, no king.

But one of them leaps out from his seat.
A portly man with what appears to be
a confident grin.
He leans over and whispers to me,
"Look at all this fun.
The plan of the universe must be good."

A snapshot of America, colors bright,
here in a sleepy town in a tavern at the dividing line.

Halfway between where I was and where I will be.

This line may appear imaginary to some.
Invisible to others.
Clear as the day's first breath of sun to me.

I know I am halfway.

Halfway between where I was and where I will be.

SONG LYRICS & POETRY

Even as a little kid,
Tom Rush had a fascination with words.
Except his interactions didn't occur
through traditional poets or outlets.

For him, it was the singers and bands
heard on Oldies radio stations and
cassette tapes played in his room.

Having to know every word being sung,
he'd sit and scribble down what he was hearing,
reading the confirmed lyrics over and over
to make sure he'd gotten them just right.

One day while listening, he wondered,
how can new songs still be written?
Hasn't everything already been written about?

That curiosity grew into an obsession
with writing lyrics of his own.

This collection is a result of that obsession.

Not everything found
in this collection is necessarily a song lyric.
Some are and have become realized through
collaborations with various musicians.
As for the rest, they're poetry of sorts.

Each is an experience had,
moment observed or story of raw realism relayed,
serving as reminders of the shared bonds between us
over love, loss, lunacy and leaving.

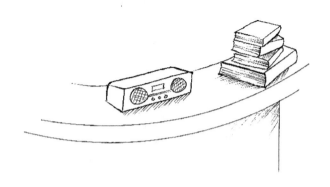

For collaborative inquiries or listening to music
by Tom Rush associated with this collection,
visit tomrushpresents.com.

Made in the USA
Middletown, DE
19 September 2021

47732210R10070